WALES
the Lie of the Land

WALES

THE LIE *of the* LAND

JEREMY MOORE *and* NIGEL JENKINS

First Impression *April 1996*

ISBN 1 85902 278 2

The Publishers wish to acknowledge the assistance of the
Design Department of the Welsh Books Council.

PRINTED AT GOMER PRESS, LLANDYSUL,
DYFED, WALES

CONTENTS

FOREWORD

'Nature in all her majesty is there; but it is the majesty of the tyrant, frowning over the ruins and desolation of a country. The enormous mountains, or rather rocks, of Merionethshire inclosed us all around. There is not upon these mountains a tree or shrub, or a blade of grass; nor did we see any marks of habitations or culture in the whole space.'

Thomas Littleton, who made an expedition to north Wales in 1755, was perhaps typical of travellers of his time when he described the mountainous areas of Wales in terms of such barrenness and desolation. Nowadays we value these features rather more than Littleton and his contemporaries appeared to do, and the Welsh landscape is renowned for aesthetic qualities which extend beyond the picturesque which he sought. The three National Parks of Wales, its Areas of Outstanding Natural Beauty and its Heritage Coasts are testimony to the value we place upon rural landscapes. And in the popular mind, Wales is still a wild place, untamed and unspoiled.

Later in his visit, Littleton climbed Moel Hebog, beneath whose summit, he wrote in his diary,

'. . .was a precipice of many hundred yards, and below a vale which though not cultivated has much savage beauty.'

Nantgwynant, below Moel Hebog, is still stunningly beautiful, perhaps the most sublime valley in the whole of Wales. But it could not be described as uncultivated, and even in Littleton's time crops such as hay, oats and barley would have been grown there, cattle and sheep grazed, and copper and probably slate mined on its northern slopes. Indeed it now really is difficult to find completely 'unspoilt' landscapes anywhere in Wales. One has to look for woodland on steep sea-cliffs and in river gorges, for example, whose inaccessibility has been their saviour. As Nigel Jenkins points out in his essay, even these will have been affected by acid rainfall and other airborne products of industrialisation. It is a fact that nearly all 'wild' country has been modified in some way in an attempt to wrest a living from it.

This, then, is 'the lie of the land', the truth behind the cliché, and the subject of this book. During my travels around Wales to complete it, my own assumptions were sometimes challenged, especially when I visited some parts of the south for the first time. My vision of the coal-mining valleys as an industrial wasteland proved to be almost completely mistaken. Barely a winding house or slag heap can now be seen, levelled with almost indecent haste; many people in 'the Valleys' live as close to Nature's doorstep as I do in mid-Wales. Perhaps I was twenty, or fifty, years too late. To be truthful, as a photographer, I would like to have seen heavy industry cheek by jowl with nature as it must once have been. But my mental images of the area were just as mistaken as those commonly held of rural Wales. The relationship between land-use and wilderness in Wales is more complex than I had originally thought.

Where industry has flourished and then died, nature does, as a rule, reclaim the land. This can take a hundred years or more; witness the lead wastelands of mid-Wales or the slate heaps of the north. The forestry industry sterilised swathes of the Welsh uplands with its monocultures of sitka spruce, but has now seen the error of its ways. While its plantations may still look awful, wildlife is slowly adapting to them and foresters are working with it and the landscape in mind. It is, in fact, probably farming that has had the most insidious and yet devastating effect on the Welsh environment and its landscape. The statistics of woodland lost, hay meadows lost, hedgerows lost, wetlands lost—to agricultural 'improvement' —particularly since the last war, are too depressing to be repeated here.

Perhaps there is something ingrained in the psyche of many farmers that, encouraged by generous subsidies from the public purse, will not be satisfied until the last vestige of 'wilderness' has been subdued or destroyed. Even now agricultural 'improvement' continues, and the same old arguments are used for keeping land under agriculture:

'when we remove agricultural usage from a piece of land, it quickly reverts to weeds and impenetrable scrub— bracken, brambles and gorse . . .'

then to birch, then oak. Where else does woodland come from? The writer continues . . .

'. . . the implications of unmanaged landscape are of an arid and uninteresting wilderness.'

We might expect these sentiments from the more extreme elements in the farming lobby, but this quotation comes, astonishingly, from an article in the *Cambrian News* by a National Trust warden in Wales. Since the introduction of intensive methods—drainage, ploughing, re-sowing, and fertilising— 'arid and uninteresting' land in these latitudes, the 'green desert' of Wales, is almost certain to be farmed in this way. Still rural, but no longer wild.

As I write these words rough grazing and wet pastures less than one mile away are being ploughed and drained for the first time ever, to the benefit of just one person—its owner, who can then graze more sheep and collect more subsidies. The fields will be emerald green all year round, attractive in winter perhaps, but the native flora and fauna will be missing. More sheep will die there, providing food for scavenging animals and birds, but this is the only benefit to the environment or the public good that will result from his work.

However, given half a chance, even the most featureless Welsh hillside would soon return to woodland. Our attempts to tame our surroundings rarely totally conceal the wilderness lying just beneath. The unpredictability of the climate should remind us of the global processes which ultimately shape life on earth. James Lovelock's 'Gaia' hypothesis suggests that the earth is an organism with an innate capacity for self-restoration no matter what—even its decline in our hands in the pursuit of short-term financial gain. We may be little more than a side-show whose survival in the process of 'recovery' is incidental.

In this book there are photographs of Wales where our presence is not apparent, scenes often referred to as 'romantic' landscapes. They have to be sought out, but they do exist, nowadays more often than not in nature reserves and other protected sites. The emphasis here is on geology, climate, and ecology. These elements are present in the photographs throughout the book but, on their own, we are led to believe,

they are not a serious subject for the photographer to tackle. In other images, human activies are unmistakable, sometimes imposed upon the wilderness layer upon layer. This, the received wisdom goes, is 'reality', and worthy of the attention of the creative photographer. But in many ways, particularly in ecological terms, the distinction between 'romance' and 'reality' is meaningless. A mountain scene is just as 'real' as an industrial landscape—and we are, in a sense, part of each. Perhaps in this case we confuse 'romance' with sentimentality'?

When I first met Nigel Jenkins he likened my photographs to the short Zen poems known as haiku; it was a comparison I had recognised, but had never spoken about. His intuitive reaction was, I felt, a good basis to commence a collaboration. And so it has turned out to be. A photographer is necessarily trapped in the present and can only hint at the past. Nigel's excellent writing fills in many of the gaps between the photographs and the history behind them.

This book is dedicated to Bill Condry, writer and naturalist, who has done so much to inspire me, both through his friendship and in his books, to explore Wales, its flora, its fauna and its beauty. He also played a critical role in the development of 'The Lie of the Land'. Many thanks.

My thanks also go to Paul Hill, Dewi Lewis, Jenny Fell, Elgan Davies and Mairwen Prys Jones of Gwasg Gomer, without whom . . . But in a strange sort of way it is also for a friend of mine, who, I swear, values nothing unless he owns it.

SNOWDON FROM GLYDER FAWR, GWYNEDD

CWM BOCHLWYD AND Y GARN, GWYNEDD

THE SUMMIT OF Y GARN (LEFT) FROM TRYFAN, GWYNEDD

GLYDER FAWR, GWYNEDD

MYNYDD DINAS, NEAR FISHGUARD, PEMBROKESHIRE

CADAIR IDRIS, GWYNEDD, FROM THE WEST

LLYN Y FAN FACH AND THE BLACK MOUNTAIN, CARMARTHENSHIRE

SNOWDON FROM BWLCH Y SAETHAU,
GWYNEDD

16

CREIGLYN DYFI BELOW ARAN FAWDDWY, GWYNEDD

CRIBYN FROM THE SUMMIT OF PEN Y FAN, BRECON BEACONS, POWYS

CARN MENYN (MEINI), PRESELI HILLS, PEMBROKESHIRE

BEDD ARTHUR AND CARN MENYN (MEINI), PEMBROKESHIRE

TRE'R CEIRI HILLFORT, LLŶN PENINSULA, GWYNEDD

CARNEDD LLYWELYN (LEFT) FROM CWM EIGIAU, GWYNEDD

LLYN PERIS AT THE FOOT OF ELIDIR FAWR, GWYNEDD

CLOGWYN STATION AND CARNEDD UGAIN, SNOWDON, GWYNEDD

TRAWSFYNYDD LAKE AND POWER STATION, GWYNEDD

MYNYDD Y CEMAIS, MACHYNLLETH, POWYS

CRAIG CERRIG GLEISIAID AND FAN FRYNYCH, POWYS

LLYN TEGID AND ARAN BENLLYN, BALA, GWYNEDD

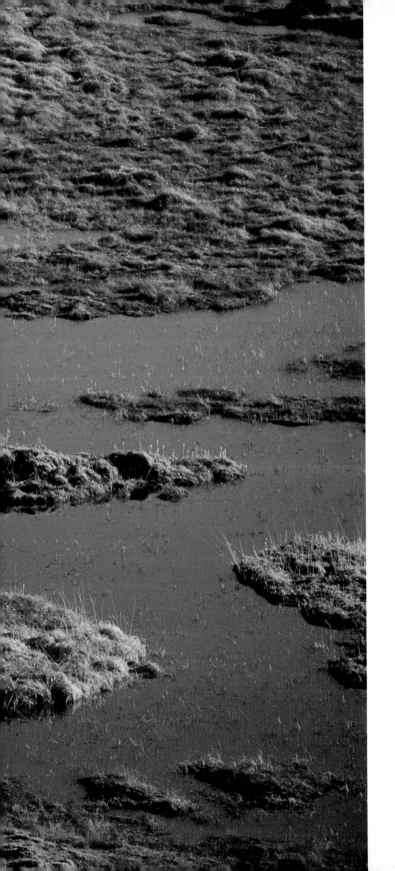

GORS LWYD, NEAR CWMYSTWYTH,
CEREDIGION

31

THE MAWDDACH ESTUARY, GWYNEDD

DYSYNNI VALLEY, NEAR TYWYN, GWYNEDD

33

THE DYFI VALLEY, LLANYMAWDDWY, GWYNEDD

LLŶN PENINSULA FROM CARN FADRYN, GWYNEDD

NEAR RHAYADER, POWYS

SOUTH OF RHAYADER, POWYS

RHEIDOL GORGE, NEAR DEVIL'S BRIDGE, CEREDIGION

CWMYSTWYTH, CEREDIGION

NEAR MACHYNLLETH, POWYS

CWMSYMLOG, NEAR PONTERWYD, CEREDIGION

NEAR LLANARTH, CEREDIGION

43

CAPEL CURIG, GWYNEDD

CASTELL TOMEN-Y-MUR, NEAR TRAWSFYNYDD, GWYNEDD

NEAR ABERDYFI, GWYNEDD

NEAR GARNDOLBENMAEN, GWYNEDD

IN THE RHEIDOL GORGE, NEAR DEVIL'S BRIDGE, CEREDIGION

RHEIDOL GORGE, CEREDIGION

NEAR MERTHYR TYDFIL

THE VALLEY OF THE RHONDDA FACH

STANLEYTOWN, RHONDDA FACH

TYLORSTOWN AND PONTYGWAITH, RHONDDA FACH

CWM BARGOED, NEAR MERTHYR TYDFIL

PENDERYN, BRECON BEACONS NATIONAL PARK

CWM LLAN ON THE SOUTHERN SLOPES OF SNOWDON

NEAR BLAENAU FFESTINIOG, GWYNEDD

ELAN VALLEY, POWYS

LLYN DINAS, NEAR BEDDGELERT, GWYNEDD

NANT BWCH, THE BLACK MOUNTAINS, POWYS

CWM EINION, NEAR TAL-Y-BONT, CEREDIGION

NEAR DOLGELLAU, GWYNEDD

THE CLYDACH GORGE, BLAENAU, GWENT

CWM EINION, NEAR TAL-Y-BONT, CEREDIGION

MAGOR MARSH, MONMOUTHSHIRE

CHIRK CASTLE GROUNDS, NEAR WREXHAM

66

NEAR TAL-Y-BONT, CEREDIGION

CORS CARON,
NEAR TREGARON,
CEREDIGION

68

NEAR ABERYSTWYTH, CEREDIGION

70

DYSYNNI RIVER, NEAR TYWYN, GWYNEDD

WYE VALLEY, WALES/ENGLAND BORDER, NEAR CHEPSTOW

DYSYNNI VALLEY, NEAR TYWYN, GWYNEDD

SNOWDON FROM MALLTRAETH, ANGLESEY

KENFIG POOL, BRIDGEND

WHIXALL MOSS, WREXHAM/CHESHIRE BORDER

76

PEMBROKESHIRE COAST WEST OF FISHGUARD

SKOMER ISLAND, PEMBROKESHIRE

CASTLEMARTIN, PEMBROKESHIRE COAST NATIONAL PARK

THE TAFF ESTUARY, CARDIFF

THE MAWDDACH ESTUARY, GWYNEDD

MARGAM, PORT TALBOT

KELP BEDS BETWEEN BORTH AND ABERYSTWYTH, CEREDIGION

84

CAERFAI BAY, NEAR ST DAVID'S, PEMBROKESHIRE

ANGLE BAY, MILFORD HAVEN, PEMBROKESHIRE

86

ST DAVID'S PENINSULA FROM RAMSEY ISLAND, PEMBROKESHIRE

RHOSILI BAY AND WORM'S HEAD, GOWER PENINSULA, SWANSEA

TREMADOG BAY FROM MOCHRAS, GWYNEDD

CARDIGAN BAY

WALES
THE LIE OF THE LAND

Nigel Jenkins

The Welsh, as O.M. Edwards famously remarked, are a nation because 'our land is unlike any other land'. Untamed Wales, a peninsula of sea-stormed peninsulas, wind-wracked, rain-lashed mountainous bastion of the tenacious Celt: such, relentlessly, is the 'image' that is peddled of the smallest and least known of the countries of Britain. But there is more to this land of Wales than meets the casual eye, for it is a realm in which, in the spirit of the legendary tales of *The Mabinogion*, all is by no means what it superficially seems.

To many, visitor and native alike, Wales's rural landscape is wild and unspoilt—and there are three National Parks to prove it. It is, though, neither truly wild nor truly unspoiled: for millenia the inhabitants of these 8,000 square miles have used and sometimes abused, shaped and remoulded the land they have lived on, as the land in turn has shaped them and helped fashion their distinctive culture—a culture in as severe a crisis today as the land, water and air that give it blood and breath.

Wales, edging clear of the shadows of heavy industry, is perhaps too beautiful for her own good. Her poets, many of them 'eco-bards' long before 'green' concerns, in the 1980s, became commonplace, keep seasoned acquaintance with their country's sometimes fatal attractions. Harri Webb (1920-94), invited to savour the delights of an Area of Outstanding Natural Beauty, dismisses its tweely perceived crags and castles as a 'beauty that is meaningless,/That's bought and sold on every side'. And R.S. Thomas (b. 1913), poet-priest of the Llŷn peninsula, challenges the consumer of scenery to look beyond the clichéd sheep 'Arranged romantically . . ./On a bleak background of bald stone' and confront 'The fluke and the foot-rot and the fat maggot/Gnawing the skin from the

small bones'. His words, like the photographs in this book, invite us to engage with the complex reality of an inhabited, worked over, ever-changing landscape, rather than mere 'scenery' that, innocent of human toil and even the busyness of natural forces, is statically, emptily 'beautiful'.

Undeniably, though, Wales is a beautiful country, and her unpredictable geography ensures frequent ambush, in even the dullest weather, by places and moments that set the spirit soaring. But how is Wales beautiful, when and for whom? Only when we unravel her shape-shifting narratives from the lie of the land do we begin to appreciate a beauty, against a history of harm, that is more than skin deep.

Humankind was not even an itch in the amphibian skull when the mountains of Wales pushed up into their primordial shape; and doubtless, given the speed with which we seem determined to burn ourselves out, they'll weather back down without us too. The mountains of Snowdonia or the louring scarps of the southern beacons might tempt us to concur with the sense of eternal immutability evoked by the poet Ceiriog's (1832-87) observation that '*aros mae'r mynyddoedd mawr*' (the great mountains forever abide). They seem to have been there from the beginning of time; but if, as we believe, the Earth was formed 4,600 million years ago, we find no trace in Wales of any rocks older than 702 million years: buried beneath younger deposits, they outcrop on Ynys Môn (Anglesey) and the Llŷn peninsula, in the borderlands and odd pockets of Dyfed. Only about 15% of the planet's story is recorded in the geology of this patch of earth which, in this current split second of terrestrial time, we Sioni-come-lately death-wise bipeds have shaped to human purposes and labelled with names. What it pleases us, for now, to call 'Cymru' or 'Wales' has been restlessly in the making since the time, 700 million years ago, when it formed part of the long-dispersed continent of Gondwanaland—along with southern Europe, Africa, India, South America, Australia and Antarctica. Originating far south of the Equator, and submerged in shallow, volcano-dotted seas, Wales glided northwards for hundreds of millions of years, a violent passage involving the deaths of oceans and collisions of continents. The view of Snowdon from Glyder Fawr on p. 8, with clouds boiling below the peaks like a frenzied primordial sea, takes the imagination back 450 million years to the mountain-making epoch when the stately heights of Snowdonia were a sulphurous archipelago of lava-belching volcanoes. Upland Wales finally broke clear of the waters a mere 65 million years ago—waters programmed by global warming to reassume, perhaps in our children's lifetime, much of Wales's lowest-lying lands.

Those mountains, having shrugged off their briny pelisse, had many changes of shape and dress still to come. In the glaciations that followed, the Welsh uplands were gouged and sharpened, churned smooth, ramparted, spilled and busted by the collosal but imperceptible violence of ice. Then the meltwaters boiled through narrow gorges, and wind and rain, sun and frost fine-tuned the transformation—a transformation that will go on until the Sun in its death throes, swollen to a red giant and devouring its children, finally gobbles up the Earth. The Welsh mountains, which have stood for many as the very embodiment of unimaginable age and permanence, are in fact mountains on the move, mere youngsters in geological terms which have yet to settle down after the upheavals of the recent ice age. While changes to the landscape by physical processes may seem to occur inconceivably slowly, in contrast with humanity's busy programmes of deforestation, quarrying, building and barraging, the landscape is capable, unassisted, of sudden and radical alteration. Folk stories about the comings and goings of mountains of sand refer to the medieval sandstorms that could obliterate whole villages, such as Cynffig (Kenfig) in Glamorgan or Niwbwrch (Newborough) in Anglesey, overnight.

About the only permanent feature of this landscape, mutating over the millenia as subtly as Welsh words mutate in different combinations, is its shiftiness. Look at a relief map of Wales and you'll see the familiar boar's head outline of her seaboard 'ghosted', in blurred focus, by two other Waleses: the sparsely populated mountainous core—that central geographical fact of Wales against which all others rest; and, out to sea, a coast-hugging mantle of paler blue, a Wales beneath the waves where no-one has lived for millenia, but among whose forests of gnarled stumps—at Borth, for instance—you may wander at low tide and hope to pluck from the muddy peat a Mesolithic hunter's flint. Beneath the waters of Bae Ceredigion (Cardigan Bay), according to a legend that has its origins in folk-memory from the Stone Age, when Wales and Ireland were joined by a land bridge, there lies the land of Cantre'r Gwaelod with its sixteen fine cities, all drowned when the drunken dyke-keeper Seithenyn's neglect of the kingdom's sea defences led to a catastrophic inundation.

There is nowhere in Wales today, no matter how remote and inaccessible, that is untouched by human hand. From the caesium fall-out of Chernobyl, which will linger in the vegetation of the north for decades to come and has rendered hundreds of farms unworkable, to the effects of acid rain on shrinking tree canopies or of man-made drought on lichens wincing into dust on unclimbable cliff faces, human activity has left its mark everywhere. Though guilt about the damage we are doing the planet may seem a new thing, our fall from ecological grace began with the onset of farming six or seven thousand years ago. In a country in which, by now, two thirds of the land have passed under the plough, no virgin or 'prelapsarian' landscapes survive; but we can get close to them in places like the raised peat bogs at Borth and Tregaron, which developed from lakes formed at the end of the last ice age, and on the islanded promontories and sea cliffs which have languished in long isolation from the human mainstream.

The earliest known 'Welsh' people were probably hunters passing through the territory when climatic conditions allowed. In a cave at Paviland in Penrhyn Gŵyr (Gower), which is accessible only at low tide, there were discovered in 1823 the bones of a young man who was ritually buried, with red ochre, shells and ivory rings, about 26,000 years ago. He and his people, dragging through the tundral cold after herds of mammoth, woolly rhinoceros and bison, were survivors on the very edge of the habitable world. To their north were the great ice-sheets whose melting, about 17,000 years ago, would turn the fertile river plain they beheld from the mouth of their cave into what we know today as the Severn Sea. Paviland man constitutes the first known burial in Britain, and was for many years the earliest hominid bone find. But he has been superseded (in Wales) by some teeth and jaw bones from a limestone cave overlooking the Elwy valley at Pontnewydd in Clwyd, a more recent find that takes us back to an interglacial period some 230,000 years ago.

The haunting corrie lake of Llyn y Fan Fach tucked beneath a frowning scarp of Mynydd Du (the Black Mountain) speaks eloquently of what happened in the ice age and its aftermath. Facing north and short of sun, like all the scarp faces of the Brecon Beacons National Park, this deep sandstone bowl was an early accumulator and late releaser of snow and ice. The lightest of summer winds, shuffling round the almost sheer 500-foot cliff, seems to whisper down the ages of the groaning and grinding of ice as it raked horizontal furrows in the rockface, and ripped away the red rubble that strews the lake's edge.

The first trees to take root when the ice relaxed its grip were the birches. And they are still here—invisible at first, but as you approach the far side of the lake you'll see their silver skins sticking out of the black peat at the water's edge. They could have been felled yesterday, but in fact they have lain here, preserved by the peat's protective juices, for upwards of 5,000 years. Yes, on the barren shores of Llyn y Fan Fach there is a birch forest, and we are padding silently through it, say, 10,000 years ago, stalking reindeer or horse. There are trees as far into the green distance as the eye can see, not only birches but oak, ash, pine, hazel. The lower the slopes, the thicker the forest. Deep, dark, impenetrable stuff. It's only down by the coast, or in the high regions where the trees are fewer, or by lakes such as this that we hunter gatherers can make a go of things. If only we could thin the forest out a bit. But we don't have the tools, there's no flint in Wales. Then— snap!—I step on a birch twig: the deer vanish and so do the boundless forests of ancient Wales. Almost no primary woodland survives into modern times, but there are isolated fragments here and there—Cwm Gwaun near Abergwaun (Fishguard), for instance, or the Cymerau, Rhygen and Ganllwyd woods in Gwynedd, or those of the Rheidol gorge, inland from Aberystwyth.

The wind-bleached moorland around Llyn y Fan Fach, pocked with sheep and shadowed by ravens, may be considered 'typical Welsh mountain wilderness' but such wastes, far from being aboriginal wildernesses, are sites of human dereliction on an almost Amazonian scale. About ten thousand years ago, as the climate grew warmer and wetter and the forests throve, Middle Stone Age food-gatherers, using hand-axes and fire, began tinkering with the trees. Though the changes they wrought in the landscape were small-scale and localised, their removal of forest cover in the damp uplands may occasionally have been a catalyst in the spread of bog mosses and the formation of peat. Then, around 4,000 BC, came the farmers, short dark giants with fields in their hands and history on their backs. These intrepid seafarers sailed in from Spain and western France to settle on the coastal fringes and along river valleys such as the Usk and Dee. They inscribed their story in stone upon the land: their monoliths jut through the heather, their cromlech capstones sail on seas of barley or meadow-grass from Gower and the Vale of Glamorgan to Pembrokeshire, Llŷn and Anglesey. The Pentre Ifan cromlech, erected on the lower slopes of the Preseli hills within sight of the Irish sea, presides over the surrounding fields like a stylised milking stool or a farmer's tweed cap, a monument to agriculture. Farming was at the revolutionary centre of Neolithic life. The cromlechs, the oldest surviving 'Welsh' buildings, were houses for the dead: here were deposited the bones of the ancestors, and from here the spirits of the tribe kept tutelary watch over the land and labours of the living. One of the Stone Age farmer's chief labours would have been felling trees to carve out plots for cultivation, and it is at this juncture that the ecological equilibrium of the nomadic earlier Stone Age begins to be lost. With their slash-and-burn clearances these farmer-pastoralists inaugurated an epoch of unprecedented human landscape-making which we are still living through today. The ecological vandalism of opencast coal mining in Glamorgan or the dumping at sea of raw sewage has its genesis in a psychology of environmental mastery that sprang from the blade of a polished stone axe over four thousand years ago.

As populations grew and technologies developed, from stone to socketed bronze and then iron axes, the reduction of virgin forest proceeded at an ever quickening pace. The stories of *The Mabinogion* (translated by Gwyn Jones and Thomas Jones, Everyman's Library 1949) may have been committed to writing in the eleventh century, but as part of the repertoire of professional story-tellers for centuries before, they open many a window on Iron Age and even earlier ways. In the first task that the giant Ysbaddaden sets for Culhwch in the tale of Culhwch's wooing of Olwen we find succinct recall of the ancient deforestations: 'Dost see the great thicket yonder? . . . I must have it uprooted out of the earth and burnt on the face of the ground so that the cinders and ashes thereof be its manure, and that it be ploughed and sown . . .'

It was the open oak and birch woodland of the higher ground that was first to be felled, terrain much easier to clear than the tangled, swampy forest of the valleys. Having selected a plot of perhaps half a dozen acres, they'd lop the branches off the trees and strip rings of bark from their trunks to kill them; when the sap had dried from the branches they would be burned where they lay, and beneath the dead, still upright trees crops would be sown. After only a few years of farming a particular patch, its fertility would be exhausted and it would be time to attack a fresh group of trees. Under the peat that now blankets the upland plateaux their stumps are still to be found.

As the climate continued to improve in the later Stone Age, these expansionist farmers pushed ever higher into the mountains; by the time Bronze Age culture arrived from central Europe in about 2,000 BC they were able to farm even further sometimes than the present upper tree limit of about 600 metres. The cairn of stones that nipples many a rounded hilltop is the Bonze Age's most prominent signature in the landscape. As communal burials in cromlechs gave way to individual cremations and interments in these mounds of rock, the 'Welsh' farmer seems gradually to have lifted up his eyes from the earth and danced his intelligence through the cosmic halls of the night sky. Locked in our noise-lit streets with a cuppola of phosphorescence 'protecting' us from the dark, most of us rarely catch a glimpse of the stars, the Milky Way being nothing more to us than a chocolate bar. You have to travel west, to the Preseli hills or the Llŷn peninsula, to find true night and a sense, beneath that ragged ribbon of stars, of our galactic home. To see it, to understand of it what can be understood—the two hundred thousand million suns, the dust, the gas, the matter factories—is both humbling and strangely empowering. 'Tonight,' you might find yourself murmuring in a field in the Preselis, 'tonight I could build Stonehenge.'

And that, in part, is precisely what the Bronze Age folk of the Preselis did. To the Bronze Age people, as to others before and after them, the Preselis were a region of profound spiritual and cultural resonance—so much so that when they built Stonehenge, which came to be recognised as the most important megalithic monument in Europe, they used some blue stones quarried at Carn Meini to form one of the henge's concentric rings. To collect and transport scores of these stones, each weighing four tons, the two hundred miles to the Salisbury Plain was indeed a monumental labour, and testament to the deep spiritual pull exerted down the ages by these numinous hills.

As we attempt to compute the ecological and human turmoil that may ensue from global warming and a likely rise in mean temperatures of two or three degrees, we have only to look back to the end of the Bronze Age to learn of the devastation brought about by a comparable alteration in what was in many ways an ideal climate. The Bronze era, with its economic surpluses, its exquisite artistry and cosmological strivings, had something about it, at least from a distance, of a golden age; but early in the first millenium BC shadows portending great change began to fall across the land.

The first of these, after 1,100 BC, was a relentless deterioration in the climate. Mean temperatures fell by almost two degrees centigrade and increased rainfall led to waterlogging, the acidification of soil and the stifling by peat of the upland acres. These farmers were no doubt coppicers and manurers, but their care for the land could hardly have included an understanding that had they felled fewer trees the waterlogging might have been reduced through transpiration. They had to abandon their sodden fields to the curlew, and resettle on lower ground. There too the rains could play murderous havoc with their lives, sending flash-floods to wash away their homesteads or silting up their valley-bottom farms. Over the course of three or four centuries they watched water undermine the very basis of their existence—as indeed too little or too much of it is doing in many parts of the world today. Small wonder that in the centuries to come the inhabitants of Wales made a god of water, anxiously offering placatory gifts at springs, lakes, rivers, wells, many of which remain sacred into modern times.

95

Then there was iron, and the wielders of iron—artful, territorial, warrior farmers. The impact on the relatively unbelligerent Bronze Agers of this awesomely hard and versatile metal, which flowed as if by wizardry from molten rock, is rememberered in a number of legends associated with lakes, including Llyn Cwm Llwch in the Brecon Beacons, Llyn y Forwyn in Glamorgan, Llyn Du'r Arddu in Snowdonia and, preeminently, Llyn y Fan Fach. The lake-god's daughter who captivates the mooning farm-boy represents an older, pre-Iron Age population driven underground in high, remote places by the war-like newcomers, and re-emerging in myth as the *tylwyth teg*, the fairy folk. The couple's love is doomed when he strikes her inadvertently with iron, the metal that shattered the Bronze Age world.

Along with iron, of course, come the Celts. Or do they? The notion that the 'Celticisation' of southern Britain was effected by a huge influx of war-crazed Gauls, Belgae and other Continentals who hammered the Bronzefolk into oblivion and refashioned the island in their own iron image has yielded to the subtler idea that it was the *culture* of the Celts that gradually crept upon the land—their religion, their customs, their language—rather than the Celts themselves in full-scale invasive person. According to this view there may have been Celts living in Britain as early as 1,000 BC, if not earlier.

The most vigorous assertion of Celtic presence in the landscape are the great hillforts whose concentric ramparts crown hundreds of hills in the semi-uplands and scores of coastal promontories. Nowhere in southern Britain possesses a greater density of Iron Age defended settlements than south-west Wales: a reminder that it was by sea and through her south and western portals that Wales received much of her prehistoric population. A massive but curiously neglected outlier of this Dyfed group of hillforts is Garn Goch which overlooks the fertile Tywi valley from a huge red shoulder of land near Llangadog. Like some other hillforts, such as the famous, and much smaller, Tre'r Ceiri on the Llŷn peninsula, there is the apparently anomalous presence within its walls of a Bronze Age cairn. This cairn seems not to have been plundered by the 'Celts' for its ready supply of building materials, but conspicuously preserved—on what may have

been a hallowed site for centuries before the 'Celts' arrived. Add such curiosities to the fact that here, as in most other British Iron Age settlements, the dwellings were circular in plan, in contrast to the rectangular form of Continental huts, and you find yourself with persuasive evidence of cultural seepage and continuity rather than violent influx and the wholesale displacement of populations. The 'Celts' who built the hillforts, from Garn Goch in the south to Tre'r Ceiri in the north, could well have been descendants of the more peaceable folk who constructed the great burial mounds. The highland peoples of Britain, aboriginals in and of the landscape rather than simply movers upon it, seem to have been great absorbers of the new, whereas those of the lowlands have been more susceptible to the cultural clean sweep.

The highlanders of Wales were Celts therefore not so much in terms of lineage and 'blood' but in terms of culture, and it was they, in communion with this unique landscape, who laid the foundations for the basic culture of the Welsh people. Though it would be long centuries yet before an identifiable Welsh nation came into being, these forbears of the modern Welsh settled, named, farmed and defended the land in patterns that are discernible and influential today. What if not a border in the making is the great chain of hillforts, most of them over 15 acres, that stretches from the Clwydian range in the north-east to Twm Barlwm in Gwent, giving notice to the denizens of the fruity 'English' plain that they mess at their peril with the men and women of the hard Welsh highlands? Not that they were conspicuously united in defence of their land: they may have shared the same language, that early form of Welsh known as Brythonic (which was spoken well after Roman times through most of the island of 'Prydain'), but they rarely spoke with one voice. Though mountains make formidable defences, they are also renowned dividers: the Welsh were, and in some ways still are, a tribal people who, having carved out their territorial patch, are inclined to negotiate unilaterally and in terms dictated by intense local loyalties. When, for instance, the Romans invaded, the Silures of south-east Wales put up a ferocious fight that lasted the best part of thirty years, whereas the Demetae of the south-west seem to have offered no resistance. The tribal divisions of Iron Age

Wales, determined to a considerable extent by the lie of the land, echo down the ages: the modern counties of Wales (in place since 1974, though reorganisation in 1996 is about to sweep them away) match uncannily the names and configurations of the ancient kingdoms.

However the names of counties come and go at governmental whim, our internal differences robustly endure, enlivening and sometimes dementing us. They tend most often to be tribally derived, whether we speak Welsh or not, from our attachment to 'y filltir sgwâr', the native square mile, and the less translatable bro (locality) within which it lies. Welsh people like to know exactly where other Welsh people are from, and who their parents are and where they are from. It is not enough to discover from a fellow's accent merely whether he's a 'Gog' (northerner, from Gogledd, meaning 'north') or one of that socially incontinent shower from 'down by there', a 'Hwntw' (from tu hwnt, meaning 'beyond'). There will be the need to establish—if he is a 'Hwntw'—whether he's from 'south Wales' or 'South Wales' (and do not doubt that murder, over that S-word, might easily be done); if he's from south-west Wales, whether he's a Turk (from Llanelli) or a Jack (from Swansea); and if he's a cowin' Jack whether he's Swansea East or Swansea West, and if Swansea West whether he's from Townhill or Tycoch, or the Uplands, where it's 'all lace curtains and no knickers' or Sketty, where sex is what they bring the coal in. In short, a sense of precisely where in the landscape a person has roots may be expected to reveal a great deal.

You have only to look out from the ramparts of a hillfort such as Garn Goch, or the sensitively reconstructed Castell Henllys in north Pembrokeshire, to understand the genesis of this brogarwch, or 'love of locality'. The Celts devoted themselves to the major task of clearing the dense low-altitude forests, tending to site their hillforts on prominences that gave them a commanding view of the arable acres below. Here, within a sweep of the chieftain's eye, lay his people's more or less self-sufficient world: a patchwork of small, irregular fields, some swaying with corn, some blue with flax, a few dotted with cattle; smoke twirling from scattered round huts, some of them hidden in the steadily shrinking clumps of forest; and—maker and sometime taker of his people's wealth—the

serpentine, shape-shifting, flood-inflicting god of a river. If you were a young man you might be sent to pass the summer months on the slopes of the higher mountain to watch over your people's sheep, goats and cattle as they fattened on the new grass of the hafod (summer place); from these heights, uninhabitable in winter, you might gaze longingly on those little dots of thatch way below, to which there would be no return until summer's end. The custom of transhumance would persist into the nineteenth century, and the ruins of later herdsmen's rough little cabins may still be stumbled on where the moorland gives way to bog or scree.

The Celtic farmer would have had to be on guard against not only the bear, boar, wolf and lynx but raiding parties from neighbouring tribes; complacency could end in ruination. If, to outsiders, the Welsh can sometimes seem defensive or over-protective of their culture it is because there has never been a time when they could afford the luxury of feeling secure: as a people 'on the edge', they have had to keep their antennae sensitively tuned to the designs of others, some of whom would gladly have pushed them over that edge. The present has invariably had to be fought for; we have never been able to take a future for granted. Or, to put it another way, in the words of Harri Webb, 'What Wales needs, and has always lacked most/Is, instead of an eastern boundary, an East Coast.'

Unlike Scotland's neat little waist of a border, with the great length of the nation stacked up behind it, Wales's sprawling belly of a frontier, which may look from the English plain like an impenetrable bulwark, is effectively no frontier at all. It is both long and riddled with gaping holes: the broad river valleys—of Gwy (Wye), Hafren (Severn), Dyfrdwy (Dee), Fyrnwy—through which invaders have been able to sweep with fatal ease. The Severn could deliver an enemy to the very slopes of Pumlumon, within fifteen or so miles of the Irish Sea, virtually cutting the nation in two.

The borderland hillforts, along with those of tactical importance in the interior, were eventually overrun by the Romans, whose conquest of the Welsh tribes (AD 47-78) proved far trickier than the subjection of the lowland people. If the Celts are by nature a people of the circle and the sinuous, contour-caressing curve, the Romans were by logic and military might a people of the straight line. Wales being a

97

country topographically inimical to straight lines, the Romans had to suffer many an uncharacteristic kink and curve in the rectangular grid of roads which they constructed to link their nodal strongholds of Caerleon, Caer (Chester), Caernarfon and Caerfyrddin (Carmarthen). We drive along many of those roads today; indeed, it was not until the mid eighteenth century that any significant additions were made to the Roman network. The most famous of their routes, sweeping from north to south, is Sarn Helen (Helen's Causeway), named perhaps not after the legendary Helen, as is often supposed, but from the Welsh for elbow, *elin,* on account of the unusual number of bends the road is forced to take. The natives, getting about on ridgeways, and using mountain crests, forest margins, cairns and stone circles as their waymarks, travelled *with* rather than against the land; the Romans treated the land, like its inhabitants, as an adversary to be overcome and stamped with their rectilinear seal—as, for instance, on Mynydd-bach Trecastell to the west of Pontsenni (Sennybridge), where, if you look down on the moorland from a helicopter, banks outlining two temporary camps look like a pair of overlapping playing cards.

The low swampy badlands of the river valleys, which tended to be no-go areas for the natives, were drained and cleared by the Romans, then roads were laid along them and arable farms established. The Romans played an imporant part in the reclamation of a huge tract of tidally submerged marshland that stretches for twenty miles along the Severn estuary, from Cardiff to the mouth of the Wye. The Gwent Levels, as these willow-fringed polders are known, are a hand-made landscape of exceptional fertility and botanical variety, despite their proximity to major conurbations and one of the biggest steelworks in Europe. Drained by a network of ditches or 'reens', some of which date from pre-Roman times, the Levels are threatened today by another bunch of machos addicted to speed and straight lines, the Department of Transport, intent on slapping a new motorway across them.

The Romans, Wales's first big industrialists, were the first serious despoilers of the land. They mined copper at Mynydd Parys near Amlwch, Ynys Môn, a tradition continued on this shattered mountain into our own time; at Dolaucothi, north of the Tywi, native slaves burrowed deep into the hillside to mine gold for their conquerors—the tunnels they worked and died in are now a tourist attraction; spoil heaps from Roman and later lead mines in mid Wales contaminated the soil and polluted rivers. From the Roman era to the present, the biggest changes in the landscape have been wrought by human hand.

Then, quicker than they had come, the Romans, after 350 years, were gone, creating if not exactly 'the Dark Ages', then a vacuum into which new invaders, and new ideas, rushed. The natives, advised by the departing imperialists to look to their own defences as Irish colonists pressed in around the coast, reappropriated what was useful to them from the past, and made a Celtic renewal of themselves. The Christianity which a handful of Roman believers had brought into Britain suddenly caught hold of the Celtic imagination, and intrepid missionaries took to muddy tracks and the western seaways to convert not only their own people but those of neighbouring Celtic lands. The hundreds of Welsh places prefixed with 'Llan' are associated invariably with one or more of this army of Celtic missionary 'saints', hardy men (usually) of God whose first base in a locality would be a simple daub-and-wattle hut with wooden palisade—the *llan* or enclosure that would in due course become the church we see today. Sometimes they would be called to test the spirit against the demands of the flesh, and would 'seek the desert' on barren summits like Carn Ingli in the Preselis or lonely cells of stone, such as St. Govan's chapel, with only the sea and a grumbling belly for companions. The Irish, who settled in large numbers in the south, became collaborators in the Christianisation of Wales: their significant cultural presence is attested by stones inscribed in the Ogam script which are to be found in various churches, north and south. The Ogam words, incised in oblique and horizontal lines down one edge of a monolith, are the earliest written form of a Celtic language; appearing sometimes in tandem with a Latin version, they might be considered our first bilingual signs.

If the Irish were absorbed, in time, by the native population, there was no absorbing the Germanic invaders from the east. What both isolated and created Wales as a distinct entity were two fateful British defeats in the late sixth and seventh centuries which drove wedges between the 'Welsh' and their fellow Britons in the West Country and Cumbria. Then a civil war in the adjacent kingdom of Mercia thrust Offa (d. 796) to the throne as the most powerful Anglo-Saxon yet, the first to style himself King of the English, and a European power with whom the Pope and Charlemagne were obliged to deal on equal terms. From the time of Penda (623-654) these pushy Anglo-Saxon frontiersmen, grabbing and trying to farm what land they could hold, had thrown up localised defences in the form of short dykes, sixteen of which are traceable today in the central March: they were to regulate passage along the ridgeways and to block off from Welsh attack the precarious valley settlements. Then, further to the north, came the thirty-eight mile Wat's Dyke, running from Treffynnon (Holywell) to Croesoswallt (Oswestry), believed to be the first effort of the Mercian state to define precisely its limits of conquest—limits which Offa was to push even further west.

The guiding principle of Offa's Dyke, behind which the invaders boxed the *Cymry* (compatriots) away and wrote them off as '*Welisc*' (foreigners) in their own land, was not that it should bristle with soldiers and weaponry throughout but that it should be Mercia's eye on Wales. Accordingly, we find that wherever possible it occupies west-facing slopes and hardly ever risks turning its back on Wales. You need to follow the Dyke on foot through the sometimes bewildering confusion of broken country over which it travels in order to appreciate the skill of its navigator and the vast ambition of the project. There had been nothing like it in these islands since Hadrian's Wall, and the Mercians were plotting it with none of the precision instruments available to the Romans.

Soldiers would have been stationed only at certain points to control trade and traffic between the two peoples, and patrols would have ridden out from garrisons such as Trefyclo (Knighton in English from *Chnichten*—town of the horsemen) to look out for Welsh trouble. There were laws to govern the Dyke including a jury system of six Welsh and six English to settle disputes, often to do with cattle raiding, a major industry for hundreds of years of this Wild West terrain.

Borders, shadow lines, a sense of 'between-ness' are familiar and sometimes painful conditions of Welsh life. But a walk down the Dyke concentrates the mind on what has made us one, a nation, in spite of our notorious internal dissensions. It invites us to recognise, in Waldo Williams's (1904-71) words,

that we have '*un gwraidd dan y canghennau*', one root beneath our many branchings. It reminds us too that less than a century after Offa had thrown up his vast earthwork—an engineering project to dwarf all others in eighth-century Europe—his almighty kingdom of Mercia had been annihilated by a combination of West Saxon and Danish invaders; we compatriots, however, are still here, if only just, twelve hundred years later.

Poetry, which qualifies Wales as immeasurably more a land of the spoken and written word than it is the fabled 'Land of Song', has always been the handmaiden of this country's history. A journey through the heroic and aristocratic court poetry of the first eight hundred years is likely to draw from the reader a sigh of 'One damn invasion after another', for between the sixth and thirteenth centuries poetry was intimately bound up with the military and political fate of the emerging nation. This was the long and gruelling age of resistance: after the Anglo-Saxons came the Vikings; after the Vikings, the Normans and the Anglo-Normans. The Vikings, in comparison with their Frenchified descendents the Normans, seem the least disruptive: they raided, they no doubt pillaged, but they also came to settle on the islands, promontories and river mouths that bear Norse names to this day—Anglesey, Bardsey, Grassholm, Skomer, Worms Head, Swansea—before following the tradition of earlier incomers and eliding smoothly with the natives. There was nothing smooth about the Normans.

Wales has more castles than any other European country, but only a few of them are Welsh castles. Possibly the most important castle in Wales is Dinefwr which stands on a bluff outside Llandeilo, overlooking the eighteenth-century park planned by Capability Brown. Like nearby Dryslwyn and Carreg Cennen, Dinefwr was built by the Welsh princes; it was the hub of power, and anti-Norman resistance, in Deheubarth, the kingdom of south-west Wales. Of the two other principal courts of medieval Wales, Aberffraw in the kingdom of Gwynedd and Mathrafal in Powys, not a stone remains standing. The smallish, sometimes idiosyncratic castles of the Welsh—Dinas Brân in silhouette high above Llangollen, the solitary tower of Dolbadarn standing sentinel at the foot of Yr Wyddfa (Snowdon)—receive nothing like the visitors who flock to the ramparts of the non-Welsh castles of Wales, the castles of our conquerors.

From the conquistadors' castles, and the towns that grew up around them, the Welsh were banned. If proof be required that the Normans, like the Romans before them, found Wales a much harder nut than England to crack—it took them two hundred years—you have only to consider the size and number of the castles they built, from Caernarfon in the north to Caerffili in the south. They are unambiguous symbols of the brute force that was necessary to crush Welsh independence. The pain of Welsh defeat is embodied to hair-raising effect in the poet Gruffudd Ab Yr Ynad Coch's (fl. 1280) cosmic howl of despair on the killing, in 1282, of Llywelyn ap Gruffudd, the last prince of independent Wales.

Happier relics of the accommodation the Welsh eventually reached with the new order are the monasteries. The Cistercians in particular, who built abbeys such as Ystrad Fflur (Strata Florida), Tintern and Valle Crucis which even in grassy ruination are hauntingly beautiful ghosts in the landscape, grew to be notable champions of Welsh civilisation; and all the monastic orders were hugely productive farmers, transforming uncultivated ground into good grazing and forests into corn fields.

Between about 1100 and 1800 the Welsh countryside as we recognise it gradually took shape. The Normans, establishing a *Wallia Anglicana* in the March and along the coastal plain, grabbed the best agricultural land for themselves, and left the natives to make what they could of the stony slopes and acid soil of the hills and mountains of *Pura Wallia*. This unequal division is reflected in the place-names and speech of the southern halves of Gower and Pembrokeshire, richly fertile farmland where English has been the dominant language for nine hundred years and from which, in Pembrokeshire's case, the Welsh were excluded by a *cordon sanitaire* of castles known as the Landsker. Gower and south Pembrokeshire, together with the spacious Vale of Glamorgan (which is really a coastal plateau), exemplify the nucleated pattern of feudal settlement that came to characterise the occupied territories: castles built to keep the restless natives at bay, manorial farming villages grown up around churches with tall and strongly embattled

towers, and fields divided into landshare strips, a few of which

survive in the arable tract at Rhosili known as the Vile.

Above the 200 metre contour line, where life continued with fewer interruptions, the typical Welsh small farm developed. George Owen of Henllys (1552-1613), writing in Elizabethan times, described a landscape of 'several and lone houses' whose main features he would surely recognise today. Villages in the uplands are comparatively few, and distances often considerable between the isolated farmsteads. The farm itself, which might incorporate an old Welsh longhouse, is usually to be found on the lowest slopes of the mountain, in a patchwork of meadows and arable fields. Ranging beyond these fields, to about 300 metres above sea level, are the *ffriddoedd,* the rough sheepwalks where the flocks pasture between spring and autumn, and the lambing, shearing and dipping are done. Beyond the long wall that divides the *ffriddoedd* from the rest of the mountain stretches the barren moorland.

There have been times when social and economic pressures have driven families to settle permanently in the formerly seasonal grazings at altitudes of 400 metres or more. Some of the remotest farms in Wales are to be found high on the eastern bulwarks of Eryri (Snowdonia), where life is a relentless battle against storms and rock, sodden peaty soils and encroaching heather. The hill farmer's age-old struggle against nature is summarised in the well-known triad:

Aur dan yr eithin,
arian dan y rhedyn,
newyn dan y grug.
[Gold under gorse, silver under fern, starvation under heather.]

From the early nineteenth century onwards, many of these high altitude farms were abandoned, leaving only a vague geometry of tumbledown walls and the odd windbreak of Scots pines that may have been able to deflect the fury of the north-easterlies, but was useless against harsher, economic gales. Sometimes you'll find an old farmstead buried deep in one of the Forestry Commission's notoriously regimented conifer plantations which, since 1919, have smothered vast acreages of moor and marginal farm land. Some ten per cent of the land of Wales is now the birdless domain of the sitka spruce and lodgepole pine.

With hundreds of hill farm workers leaving the industry every year, the crisis of rural Wales continues. Not only individual farms but, now, whole farming regions are close to collapse. The blight afflicts the lowland farms too. In Gower, I have watched a farm I love broken up into a cluster of meaningless plots for jaded city types who want a few acres on which to play the farmer. They harrow their fields not to keep the grass in good heart but to give their property the appearance of a neatly striped suburban lawn; no one uses or remembers the resonant, history-laden names of the fields.

Mention 'Wales' and 'industry' together, and most people think of the heavy extractive and manufacturing industries of the south. To many unacquainted with the country, Wales amounts to little more in their imaginings than coal and Tom Jones, the two most famous Welsh exports. But contrary to popular perceptions, the modern industrial era began perhaps with greater vigour in the north than in the south. Copper mining burgeoned anew on Anglesey in the 1760s, and Thomas Pennant (1726-98), writing at about that time, described Flintshire as 'black with smoke' from the lead and copper undertakings that, with coal mining, dominated the economy of his home county. Above all, of course, there was slate, north Wales's industry of industries, which has carved enduring monuments to itself in the pyramidal 'benches' of the massive quarries at Dinorwig and Penrhyn, and the colossal tonnages of waste through which the houses of Blaenau Ffestiniog and Corris peep like moles. Slate was mined in north-west Wales from medieval times, but it was not until the mid-eighteenth century that the industry took off, establishing itself by the 1860s as the most important of its kind in the world. No extractive industry has wrought more dramatic alteration to the Welsh landscape than slate.

It was not until the early nineteenth century that the industrial activity of mid and north Wales began to be overshadowed by the spectacular growth of the coal-based industries in the south, that reached from Llanelli to the eastern valleys of Gwent.

Wales, it has been plausibly argued, is where the world's industrial civilisation began, and it is ultimately to south Wales that we look to find 'South Wales' and the crucible of the Industrial Revolution. In transforming the world, the Industrial Revolution also, of course, radically altered Wales and left seemingly indelible signatures on the landscape. As the novelist Gwyn Thomas (1913-1981) observed of his ravaged Valleys, 'Society and nature have come together to achieve some amazing patterns, and they should be told not to do it again.'

Coal was not a significant player in that revolution's precursory rumblings. It was wood that they used for smelting copper and iron in places like Neath and Tintern in the sixteenth and seventeenth centuries. As the timber was exhausted in one area, they would dismantle their furnaces and rebuild them next to a new tract of forest. A famous poem by 'Anon.', translated by Gwyn Williams (1904-90), laments the destruction of Glyn Cynon Wood in Glamorgan:

Many a birch tree green of cloak
(I'd like to choke the Saxon!)
is now a flaming heap of fire
where iron workers blacken.

By 1717 copper was being smelted at Glandŵr (Landore), Swansea. Within less than a hundred years Swansea would become a metallurgical centre of world importance and, effectively, the economic capital of Chile, whence the copper ore was imported. It is perhaps difficult to recall that the Lower Swansea Valley, where today the Swansea Hilton reposes beside an ornamental lake, was not so long ago the most polluted landscape in Wales. George Borrow (1803-81), touring 'Wild Wales' in 1854, stood transfixed by the 'accursed pandemonium' of smoke, filth and fire that he beheld from the valley side. 'So strange a scene I had never beheld in nature,' he wrote. 'Had it been on canvas, with the addition of a number of diabolical figures . . . it might have stood for Sabbath in Hell . . . and would have formed a picture worthy of the powerful but insane painter Hieronymous Bosch.'

Coal, which had been mined in only a desultory fashion before about 1750, became crucial to this explosion of industrial activity: no coal, no Industrial Revolution. Coal was, and still is, mined in north-east Wales, but it was the great kidney-shaped basin of the south Wales coalfield, stretching from Pontypool in Gwent to St. Bride's Bay in Pembrokeshire, that powered the extraordinary frenzies of 'Copperopolis', the massive iron foundries of Dowlais and Merthyr, and the pioneering developments in steel and tinplate which eventually overtook iron. From 1830 coal was mined for export, to fuel industries and drive ships all over the world. This coal, this extraordinary hoard of fossilised peat, compounded of tropical swamps some 300 million years ago, made poverty-stricken Wales rich overnight. Or rich enough, at any rate, to retain most of her population, and thereby her culture, when other less naturally endowed countries were losing thousands of their people to the chancy sea-paths of emigration. Life in rural Wales could be unremittingly hard: country people, reduced to landless destitution by unofficial enclosures, often saw a better life for themselves among the smoke and noise of the coalmines and foundries, and flocked to the industrial south, in a memorable phrase, 'to seek their freedom' from the shackles of near and sometimes actual poverty in their sheep-bitten hills. Indeed, it was to south Wales, as well as to America and Australia, that thousands of outsiders—Spanish, Italian, Irish, English—flocked to find a living.

The phenomenal scale and speed of this in-rush brought a whole new Valleys society and landscape into vibrant being: the terraced housing stretching in long ribbons either side of the narrow valley, the miners' institutes, the pubs and chapels trying to outnumber each other, the pit-head wheels and winding gear, the sprawling black cones of waste, and always, near at hand, that other world, to quote Gwyn Thomas, 'just up the hillside over the ridge [of] a pastoral calm that has never seriously been breached.' King Coal, to be sure, was a hard and unpredictable master but his coffers were there for the plundering; their depth and width seemed endless. The promised land of socialism appeared to fill the sky beyond the mountain with a blood-red glow.

But it all turned out, in the poet Idris Davies's (1905-1953) words, a 'dream and swift disaster'. Coal crashed, the General Strike of 1926 ended in defeat for the miners, and the Depression years that followed brought such hunger and poverty that nearly half a million of the Welsh were driven permanently out of their country.

Wales, since then, has been trying to adjust to the relentless decline and near extinction of her traditional heavy industries. The industrial era concentrated a majority of Wales's population, which for most of her history rarely exceeded a quarter of a million, in the Valleys and coastal towns of the south, and it is here still that you will find three quarters of the population of 2,913,000. The re-greening of the Valleys, which has been under way for nearly thirty years, was set in train by two social calamities: the collapse of that coal-tip at Aberfan in October, 1966 which killed 116 children and twenty-eight adults, and stung the Government into action against a degraded and dangerous environment; and the dereliction, after the phoney 'boom years' of the 'fifties, of south Wales's coal- and steel-based economy. Salmon may swim upstream through Cardiff, against waters that once ran black with slurry, and fresh turf may cover the landscaped tips, but the poverty, ill health and despair that result from chronic unemployment are festering scars on the Valleys landscape that no amount of half-baked and deceitful Government 'initiatives' can grass over.

As we seem to go back in time to a greener Valleys environment so we return, in places like Cwm Nedd (the Neath Valley), to a pre-modern world of tin-pot private mines lost among the trees, operated by three men and a pony (see p. 54). But before we have time to wax sentimental about apparent returns to 'good old small-scale ways', we catch the roar downwind of heavy machinery and see dust drifting up from the other side of the valley: the big deep mine may have all but disappeared, but it is being replaced by opencast mining: this has been described by the House of Commons Select Energy Committee as 'one of the most environmentally destructive processes being carried out in the UK.' Unhindered by any statutory 'ceiling' on opencast activity, the coal companies are forging ahead, while the political climate lasts, with a massive programme of expansion; nowhere between south Pembrokeshire and Blaenavon may be considered safe from their attentions; the Mold-Buckley-Wrexham region in the north-east is also a targeted area. Mid and west Glamorgan currently bear the brunt of opencasting's ruinous assault on the environment, and local opposition is increasingly vigorous and articulate. Wales Against Opencast, one of the fastest growing single-issue campaign groups, is uniting English- and Welsh-speakers alike in a struggle to save a wide range of sensitive woodland and greenfield sites from obliteration in the cause of 'cheap' energy. The imaginative direct action tactics of groups such as Earth First! have been welcomed lately by frontline campaigners, ensuring that the rapacious short-termism of a deregulated and privatised coal industry is likely to meet with ever stiffening resistance.

It is on the southern coastal strip that most of what is left of Wales's heavy industry survives, in the steelworks at Newport, Port Talbot and Llanelli, the oil refineries at Milford, the petrochemical works at Baglan and Llandarcy (the only 'Llan' named after an industrialist, one D'Arcy); they have been joined in recent years by the big engineering and microelectronics 'inward investors' from Germany, North America and Japan whose large manufactories hang like garish postmodern jewels from the necklace of the M4 motorway. One expects in rural Wales to be struck by epiphanies, but there's a terrible beauty to be found in industrial Wales too— the luminescent fantasia of Baglan at night, or the sun striking through bundling grey clouds to turn some filth gusting from a smokestack into a wing of silver against the blackly green hills.

The coal-created ribbon settlements of the Valleys have altered less in recent years than towns with more space to expand. Almost every small town with room to manoeuvre has fallen for the fashionable (and uniformly ugly) town's-edge retail sheds and shopping malls which, it has been realised too late in the day, have done lethal damage to the traditional shopping 'ecology' of the High Street. They have also been catalysts in the suburbanisation and itchy-fingered 'improvement' of our towns, a process which has reduced many of them to restlessly transmuting environments bereft of identity and meaning.

The same destructive suburbanising mentality is at work, if less obviously, in rural and coastal Wales, which are the regions most heavily exploited by Wales's major 'replacement' industry, tourism. It is hardly a new industry. The first tourists were no doubt the soldiers of the Roman army, who can

scarcely be considered a benign presence. Much later came a gentler, less intrusive visitor, the eighteenth- or nineteenth-century searcher after the 'picturesque' and 'sublime' and quirky Celtic exotica. Dr. Johnson may not have taken to our 'horrid mountains' and 'wretched hovels', but others on their 'Cambrian tours' found much to admire and wrote memorably of their travels in accounts that advertised the delights of this strange land to similarly adventurous (and well-heeled) spirits. They came, and they went, these early tourists, in their hundreds rather than hundreds of thousands, leaving little more to mark their passing than a signature scrawled in sand. Not so, of course, the twentieth century visitors whose combined impact can be as corrosive of the language and culture of Wales as of her landscape and ecology. Until as recently as the 1940s my native Gower was a virtual agricultural independency, with its own languages (Welsh and the Gower dialect), strong local identity and mutually dependent social relationships. But in the 1950s the Gower that exists now only in the memories of isolated pensioners began to break up and disappear under the joint pressures of suburbanisation and mass tourism. Every fine weekend throughout the summer Britain's first Area of Outstanding Natural Beauty is, like similar honey pots all around the coast, one gigantic traffic jam, so overcrowded that it is impossible for the visitor, no matter how interested in what is left of the culture, to connect with any sense of indigenous life. And when the crowds leave, having experienced little more than crowds, the stigmata of their passing are writ large in the landscape: the sand dunes trampled down, the cliff-top paths gouged into broad, beaten-earth highways. Leisure, it is increasingly acknowledged, now threatens to supersede labour as the biggest despoiler of the countryside.

Wales is heavily dependent on tourism. The industry brings £1.3 billion into the economy, nearly 40% of it being spent in the Welsh-language heartland of Gwynedd, and it generates 95,000 full-time jobs. As the poet and environmental critic John Barnie (b. 1941) has noted, 'A nation that depends on tourism as Wales now does must learn to manipulate its culture . . .'

It manipulates its culture by confecting and marketing 'images' of Wales that draw shamelessly on all the flattering old clichés while carefully avoiding the 'downbeat' and complexly angular. One awkward fact the 'spin doctors' would rather was kept from troubling the sleep of visitors is the problem of depopulation and in-migration. Wales has recently suffered a huge demographic upheaval of which few seem to have taken much notice. It has been calculated that during the 1980s half a million mostly Welsh people, a sixth of the population, moved out of Wales, and half a million mostly non-Welsh people moved in. An equivalent upheaval in England would involve eight million Englishmen leaving dear old Blighty to be replaced by eight million Frenchmen.

The magnet, of course, is the relative tranquillity and apparently 'unspoilt' nature of the land of Wales. As for the Welsh language and culture, many incomers who may not be aware initially of the existence of such things, take pains to discover what country they are in, and make generous and valuable contributions to contemporary life, becoming in due course what the historian Gwyn A. Williams (1925-95) hailed as 'the New Welsh'. Others, alas, do not, electing as mere consumers of lovely scenery to remain indifferent to the people, their languages and ways of being—an ignorance that is shared, it has to be admitted, by not a few natives.

Holidaymakers drawn back to Wales as wealthy retirees or second-home owners tend to settle in 'the most beautiful' parts of Wales which are often in the culturally sensitive *bro Gymraeg* (Welsh-speaking areas). Those displaced by the arrival of this leisured superstratum in the depopulating heartland tend to be former workers of the land with deep family roots; if removed in large numbers their disappearance is as damaging to the 'cultural ecology' as the obliteration of ancient beeches by road building might be to the ecology of a place like the Clydach gorge.

Violent alteration to the physical environment invariably lays waste to the cultural. Wales has scores of natural lakes: there are sixty in Snowdonia alone. Most of them are small, and even the few big ones, such as Llyn Tegid (Bala), are harmoniously in scale with their surroundings. But there are new lakes in Wales—Claerwen, Clywedog, Celyn—some of which, to the historically attuned sensibility, rather than that of the merry jet-skier, are sharply disharmonious places. Llyn Celyn above all, sometimes known as Llyn Tryweryn,

exemplifies the shameful fate of farms and villages that were drowned, in spite of unanimous public opposition, to supply an English city with water. By flooding Cwm Tryweryn and the village of Capel Celyn in the 1960s, the bureaucrats of Liverpool Corporation destroyed unthinkingly, in the words of Bobi Jones's (b. 1929) poem, 'The cynghanedd and the ballads, the close society and the prayer/They could never see at all . . ./. . . the aristocratic spacious thing,/The treasure not hidden at all in any other place—/The warm priceless life . . .' The authorities claimed in hurt dudgeon that Liverpool needed the reservoir to supply drinking water, but later admitted the water was for 'industrial expansion and re-sale at a profit.'

Water, as Flann O'Brien's fictitious 'authority' De Selby wisely proclaimed, is rarely absent from any wholly satisfactory situation. And it is water that is increasingly the focus of environmental campaigns, from the struggle against the reckless experiment of barraging river mouths, to Surfers Against Sewage, from the world against acid rain, to Friends of Cardigan Bay against oil and gas exploration of the west Wales coast, which threatens the habitat of a rare colony of bottle-nose dolphins, and much else besides. Harri Webb, in a beautiful hymn to oceanic variety called 'The Flocks of the Moon', warns careless humanity to heed the silent music of the sea-moving moon:

There is no end to her wonders
Yet all are so frail, so frail.
The earth spills poison,
Cities vomit filth,
Soon it may be too late,
The flocks of the moon all die,
Her dancers rot,
Her music vain.
Still she will drag the dead weight of the tides,
No longer an enchantress but a drudge,
An old crazed witch with a blank face
Who will curse to kill
And you too will die.

Humanity, his poem implies, is in this mess together, and

there are few unilateral solutions to what are invariably global problems.

As we contemplate our long denuded mountain ridges, bristling here and there with the latest indignity we have inflicted on them, stark forests of noisy wind turbines, we might call to mind the shrinking rain forests of the Amazon, or the galloping deserts of Africa, or the deluged flatlands of Bangladesh. Cushioned in the overfed and self-indulgent west from the more extreme consequences of human over-extension, we nevertheless owe responsibilities to such places.

The world is one blue teetering orb, and everyone wants to save the whales; a few of us, living on this particular swath of it, live in hope also of saving Wales, in all her cultural, topographical and ecological variety. There are signs that we are learning at last the harsh lesson of Tryweryn and other sites of environmental and cultural defeat: that if we don't take responsibility for our own bruised acre of the planet, no one else will; and that abdicating such responsibility hardly fits us for making ourselves useful globally.

Wales has a long tradition of robust popular protest, from Glyndŵr's valiant attempt to restore Welsh independence in the fifteenth century to Cymdeithas yr Iaith's (the Welsh Language Society) daubing of English-only road signs in the 'sixties and 'seventies which eventually persuaded the Government to adopt a bilingual policy. There have been notable successes on the environmental front. In the 1940s, for instance, the people of the Preselis successfully resisted Ministry of War plans to turn their sacred hills into a tank training range. The people of Hirwaun in the 1970s refused to allow two large gas tanks to be built near their homes. The

huge reservoir of Llyn Brianne, to the north of Llanymddyfri (Llandovery), whose construction involved no dispossessions, is a tribute to the protesters of Cwm Gwendraeth Fach, whose valley to the south-east of Carmarthen was threatened with inundation—until they decided to put a stop to the scheme, as a poem by David Hughes (b. 1948) recounts:

> When Cwm Gwendraeth Fach was to be put to flood
> The people, knowing water is thinner than blood,
> Chained gates, drove machinery into gaps.
> The civil engineers rolled up their maps.

A victory as this was for grass-roots resistance, few anticipated at the time the devastation that Llyn Brianne would visit on the habitat of Rhandir Mwyn, where several unique species have been lost to the world forever.

For every Cwm Gwendraeth Fach there seems to be a Tryweryn; for every Preseli mountainside saved from the bombardment of tanks there seem to be huge tracts of Wales—the clifftops at Castlemartin, or Mynydd Epynt in south Powys—lost indefinitely to the war machine.

Our old tribalist tendencies ensure that between our vigorously fought local campaigns and our concern for global issues there is a missing link: a care for the land of Wales as a whole. Perhaps, at last, we are beginning to learn unity, and the time is approaching when we will take responsibility on Welsh terms for the economy, varied habitats and diverse culture of Wales. Then that foggy thing, a Welsh nation, might truly come into connection with the world, and cease to be mistaken for yet another lie of the land.

PHOTOGRAPHER'S NOTES

Page 8/9

Probably the most magnificent day I have ever had in the Welsh mountains. At about 750 metres I emerged from dank cloud into brilliant sunshine. Even on this February day it was shirt-sleeve weather on the summits. Another photographer I met had used fifteen rolls of film. But the joy of being up there on such a tremendous day was almost my downfall. Starting the descent near sundown, I very quickly plunged into the darkness beneath the sea of cloud. Fortunately I met two other walkers who had a torch, and with my map we navigated our way safely to the road together.

Page 20

One hot June evening I took my camera and sleeping bag onto the rounded hills of Preseli. As dusk fell a breeze from Cardigan Bay brought mist to swirl around the summits and among the stones. Unfortunately, I had forgotten my tripod and one of my cameras jammed. Definitely one instance where being a photographer spoils the experience of 'being there'.

Page 21

Archaeological remains and native grassland such as this, with its native flora and fauna, often owe their survival to the common land upon which they stand. With its complex system of grazing and other rights, agricultural improvement is difficult on common land, although it is usually overgrazed.

Page 24

The hollowed out mountain of Elidir Fawr is home to the Dinorwig hydro electric power station.

Page 25

This is probably my favourite building in the whole of Wales, perched on the edge of a precipice at an altitude of 750 metres. It houses ticket issuer, point changer and door slammer at Clogwyn station on the Snowdon Mountain Railway. One day there were a dozen or so railwaymen in and around the station, all eating bacon and sausages fried on the top of its stove.

Page 26

The nuclear industry is the major exception to the rule that once industry has declined, nature gradually reclaims the land. Trawsfynydd nuclear power station, situated bang in the middle of the Snowdonia National Park did provide work for some local people. Now its useful life is over but it is, we are told, too radioactive to be dismantled until the 22nd century. Future generations may pay dearly for our 'nuclear experiment'.

Page 27

Probably the most controversial issue in rural Wales at the moment is the development of wind farms, and I have mixed feelings about them. On a number of occasions I have turned a corner to see a windfarm on a hilltop and felt my heart jump with joy. Clean Energy! They may disfigure the landscape but any more or less than the drab blankets of conifers already draped over so many Welsh hillsides? But if the economics of wind energy are examined more carefully their benefits are more doubtful. Not only do they contribute a very small proportion of our overall electricity requirement, but the main beneficiaries appear to be the multi-national construction and power companies who collect the government subsidies. Why not invest in energy efficiency first?

Page 28

Sheep can look very picturesque but in the large numbers found in Wales they are a very destructive force within the landscape. Their grazing prevents woodland regeneration and reduces botanical diversity. When grassland is 'improved' to increase sheep numbers, a mix of native species is replaced with a grass monoculture whose value to the environment is virtually nil. Much of rural Wales is, in fact, little more than a sheep ranch. Sheep farmers in many parts of Wales receive 50% or more of their income from the public purse but the public has little or no control over what they do.

Page 37

As a photographer I often find myself wishing I was somewhere else either in space or time. On this foggy and frosty December day I reached the brow of a hill and looked down into the valley below me. I knew I was in the right place, for once, at the right time.

Page 38
From the exhibition 'After the Wildwood'. The forestry plantation on the skyline was probably planted to remain below it. The oak woodland is as near to 'wilderness' as anything else in Wales.

Page 43
These scrawled slogans advertise a 'nature walk' which was once open to the public, but is now surrounded by an eight foot barbed wire fence. Entry to it is by turnstile, at a cost of £1 per person.

Page 45
Castell Tomen-y-Mur, a Norman motte and bailey situated within an extensive Roman fort, the former built some one thousand years after the latter was abandoned.

Page 50
I 'discovered' this valley during the final stages of work on *The Lie of the Land* . Cwm Bargoed lies just a few miles south-east of Merthyr Tydfil, arguably the cradle of the industrial revolution in Wales. But with its extensive alder and other woodland, and its lightly grazed grassland it recalls a pre-industrial era in 'the Valleys'. Astonishingly, it receives no protection under the Wildlife and Countryside Act; one change of ownership and we could lose this gem to agricultural 'improvement'. The private coal mine pictured on page 54 lies in the top right hand corner of this photograph, with Cwm Bargoed coal washery on the skyline. Surely the open-cast coal industry has its greedy eyes on this pristine landscape too.

Page 53
I arrived here early one April morning. As I was looking around for the best viewpoint (I ended up perched precariously on top of a gatepost), a local man began chatting, as south Wales people do. He told me that photography students are often brought to this spot. I wonder what their photographs are like.

Page 55
On a visit to that very interesting country between the Heads of the Valleys and the Brecon Beacons National Park, I passed this limestone quarry, and immediately saw a photographic opportunity. Setting up my tripod just outside the quarry entrance (the first pair of oil drums) I immediately attracted the attention of quarry workers. First a man in overalls came over, and he, no doubt, reported back to his superiors, because a man in a shirt and tie appeared a few minutes later. What was I doing? 'Well, I'm a landscape photographer, and I just happened to be passing . . .' I told him. He told me he thought I might have been one of those anti-quarry campaigners. 'Well, yes, I could be,' I said.

Page 58
Conifers reflected on the surface of Pen-y-Garreg reservoir.

Page 63
This gorge, a National Nature Reserve within the Brecon Beacons National Park, with its magnificent native beech woodland, is threatened by plans to widen the Heads of the Valleys road which runs parallel to it. The river itself is polluted from two sources at this point; the main watercourse by sewage discharged upstream, the tributary on the left by iron compounds from abandoned mines nearby.

Page 64
This valley was once described as 'temperate rainforest' by the biologist and environmentalist David Bellamy.

Page 66
The tiny light sources in the foreground are dew droplets backlit by the low morning sun.

Page 70
This graffiti was shown to me by the farmer, who claimed to have carved it when he was a small boy. It reads 'Herr Adolf Hitler 1933' and is dated 1937. It includes a large swastika. I was advised to exclude the photograph from the exhibition 'After the Wildwood' to avoid causing offence.

Page 79
Part of the tank ranges on the spectacular limestone coast of

south Pembrokeshire. Public access is largely forbidden but, ironically, the presence of the army has allowed the native grassland, rich in wild flowers, to survive. Under agriculture, it would have been ploughed up many years ago.

Page 82/83

After failing to locate the heavy industry I had hoped for in 'the Valleys', I headed for Port Talbot. I knew I would find it there. Walking along the foreshore, where the public normally has access, I was approached by a security guard who called his superior. There followed a long discussion about my being there. 'It is British Steel Policy,' I was told, several times, 'to confiscate the film of any photographer found on its property.' I politely declined to hand over any film, and decided to risk the consequences, which might have included the police, I was told. I quickly walked across the beach, where this wonderful scene quickly revealed itself. My brush with security ended happily enough. Soaked to the skin by sleet and hail, I headed back to the shore, where the official was waiting for me in his car. Not for further interrogation, as I feared, but to drive me off the site, by now happy about my intentions and glad, no doubt, to get me out of his hair.

Page 84

Kelp just offshore at low tide. Cardigan Bay is of exceptional wildlife interest, with its breeding and wintering birds, its 'sarnau' (shingle ridges running offshore at right angles to the shore, believed to be unique), and its bottlenose dolphins. Since 1989 Friends of Cardigan Bay has been campaigning for its protection, most recently against oil exploration.

Page 86

In late February 1996, the *Sea Empress* ran aground at the mouth of Milford Haven. Following a bungled salvage operation, an estimated 70,000 tons of crude oil poured into the sea, polluting the coastline for many miles.

The Government has awarded licences to explore for oil as close as two miles from the Pembrokeshire coast.

Glossary

The following Welsh words are commonly contained in place-names. Knowing their meanings will help in identifying sites.

aber	estuary, confluence
bach/fach	small, lesser
caer/ceiri	fort(s)
carn/garn	rock, cairn
carnedd	cairn, tumulus
cors/gors	marsh
craig	rock
cwm	valley
fan (from *ban*)	peak
llan	church enclosure
llyn	lake
mawr/fawr	great, big
mynydd	mountain, moorland
nant	brook
pen	head, top, end
pont	bridge
tre	homestead, hamlet, town